Look Out by the Water

Acknowledgments

Executive Editor: Diane Sharpe

Supervising Editor: Stephanie Muller

Design Manager: Sharon Golden

Page Design: Rafi Mohamed

Photography: Greg Evans International: pages 7, 23; Chris Fairclough: pages 19, 25; Alex Ramsay: cover (middle right), page 21; Tony Stone: cover (left, top right), pages 9, 15.

ISBN 0-8114-3737-X

Copyright © 1995 Steck-Vaughn Company.

1 2 3 4 5 6 7 8 9 00 PO 00 99 98 97 96 95 94

STECK-VAUGHN
READ ALL ABOUT IT

Look Out by the Water

Helena Ramsay

Illustrated by
Colin King

STECK-VAUGHN
COMPANY
ELEMENTARY · SECONDARY · ADULT · LIBRARY

You should always be with a grown-up when you are at a beach. Never go by yourself.

The ground is often slippery near water. If you run, you might fall and hurt yourself.

7

Always behave when you are at a beach or a pool. If you don't, you could get hurt.

Never jump or dive into water
unless you know how deep it is.

Always find a safe place to
get in and out of the water.

Come over here,
and get in with us.

It's safe here.
We can see the bottom.

12

In the ocean, the water can get deep very quickly. Be careful never to go in too deep.

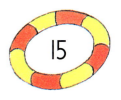

The current in the ocean can be
very strong. If you got in too deep,
the current could pull you away.

It can be dangerous at the ocean.
Sometimes rescue boats have to
help people in trouble.

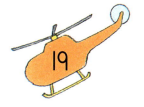

19

There's a strong current in rivers, too.

When you throw sticks in the water, it carries them away.

20

Swimming in rivers can be very dangerous.

Once the current carried my toy boat away.

The ocean tide can come in very quickly.

When the tide comes in, don't go too far out in the water.

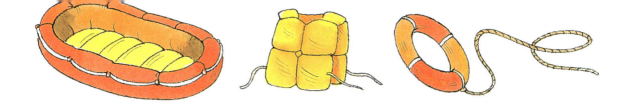

People of all ages should wear a
life jacket when they go on a boat.

Water can be dangerous, even if
you know how to swim.

25

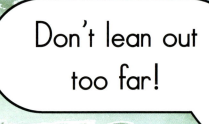

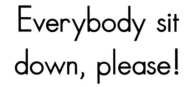

On a boat, always do as
you are told so you don't fall
in the water.

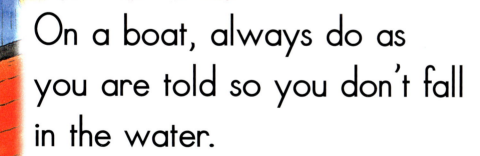

We had a great day!

So did I.
You have all been
very good.

Always be careful near water,
and you will have lots of fun.

Some of these children are being careful, and some are not. Do you know which ones are which?

Index

Beach **4-5, 9**

Boats **18-19, 24-25, 26-27, 28**

Currents **17, 18-19, 20-21**

Depth **11, 14-15, 16-17, 23**

Diving **10-11**

Jumping **10-11**

Life jacket **24-25**

Ocean **14-15, 17, 18-19, 22-23**

Raft **18**

Rescue boat **18-19**

River **20-21**

Swimming pool **8-9, 16**

Tide **22-23**

Tide pool **4, 6-7**